RE 615H SOUTH AMERICAN CICHLIDS

Distributed in the UNITED STATES by T.F.H. Publications, Inc., 1 TFH Plaza, Neptune City, NJ 07753; on the Internet at www.tfh.com; in CANADA by Rolf C. Hagen Inc., 3225 Sartelon St., Montreal, Quebec H4R 1E8; Pet Trade by H & L Pet Supplies Inc., 27 Kingston Crescent, Kitchener, Ontario N2B 2T6; in ENGLAND by T.F.H. Publications, PO Box 74, Havant PO9 5TT; in AUSTRALIA AND THE SOUTH PACIFIC by T.F.H. (Australia), Pty. Ltd., Box 149, Brookvale 2100 N.S.W., Australia; in NEW ZEALAND by Brooklands Aquarium Ltd., 5 McGiven Drive, New Plymouth, RD1 New Zealand; in SOUTH AFRICA by Rolf C. Hagen S.A. (PTY.) LTD., P.O. Box 201199, Durban North 4016, South Africa; in JAPAN by T.F.H. Publications. Published by T.F.H. Publications, Inc.

MANUFACTURED IN THE
UNITED STATES OF AMERICA
BY T.F.H. PUBLICATIONS, INC.

FINDING A NICHE

Cichlids (pronounced *sick-lids*) are fascinating to tropical fish hobbyists for a number of reasons. They also have a particular appeal to ichthyologists and ethologists (those who study animal behavior). That is because they are biology's shining example of one family of fish (Cichlidae-pronounced *sick-lid-DEE*) being able to adapt to so many different niches and developing so many different species. The reasons for this success have been postulated by scientists, but they remain somewhat speculative. Some of the reasons for success generally agreed upon by biologists are that cichlids are intelligent for fish, and this appears to be an advantage. Also, cichlids care for their young in some manner. That is, they protect them, and they often feed them, not to mention keeping them clean and supplied with oxygenated water. Various species use different methods, but all this protection for the young is an obvious advantage, even though the parents must pay a price for it. The final reason agreed upon is that cichlids, along with the very similar marine damsels (and the also similar wrasses, surfperches, and parrotfishes), have two sets of

A firemouth cichlid protecting its young.

teeth, one in the jaws and one in the throat. Many species of fish have one or the other, but only these groups have both. The advantage in this is that each set of teeth can be evolved for a separate task, thus making the species more adaptable to changing situations.

Obviously, the intelligence and the care for the young is the type of thing that would appeal to people who want to keep tropical fishes. As a bonus, cichlids are quite colorful. Some of the most colorful species are found in the Great Lakes of Africa. For that reason, cichlids from those lakes have been extremely popular. They are still the most popular of the cichlids, but advanced aquarists have in recent years begun taking a particular interest in the cichlids of South America. To understand the reason for that, we need to understand the cichlids of the rest of the world and how they are different from their South American brethren.

Cichlids are found in Africa, Madagascar, the south of India, and in the tropical regions of the Americas, including some of the islands in the Caribbean Sea, like Cuba, not to mention in parts of the ocean itself.

As I mentioned before, some of the most colorful cichlids are found in the Great Lakes of Africa. In fact, cichlid species dominate those lakes in terms of numbers of species. The lakes are like giant

Cichlids originated in marine environments. There are still cichlid-like fishes in the oceans, like this *Pomacentrus bankenensis.*

PHOTO BY ROGER STEENE.

The brown discus, *Symphysodon aequifasciata axelrodi.*

PHOTO BY DR. HERBERT R. AXELROD.

Africa in which vast supplies of algae grow. Cichlids are the only fish that have found a way to get the algae. No fish could adapt to such hot water, but cichlids developed a certain immunity to it so that they could take it for short durations, as they made quick forays into the territory when currents of cool water helped ameliorate the situation. The point is that cichlids are amazingly adaptable wherever they are. And in South America, it is believed that they had at least 50 million years in which to make the adaptations, while in the Great Lakes of Africa, they have only had about three million years in the opinion of most scientists (ichthyologists and geologists, the latter estimating the age of the lakes).

Apparently, cichlids found unexploited or little-used feeding niches in South America and then moved from them to areas of extreme specialization. Thus, we have the round and extremely compressed discus, which lives in areas in which there is almost no food for baby fish to eat. The cichlid's solution in this case was to develop a food to keep the fry alive and growing until they could feed upon what was available for larger fish babies. Discus, therefore, secrete (both parents) a specialized food from their skin for the young to feed upon. The parents take turns in feeding the fish, and one parent can flick the young to its mate when depleted of the "fry food" resource.

So bizarre and different are discus, and the somewhat similar

Discus fry feeding from the sides of the parent.

PHOTO BY HANS JOACHIM RICHTER.

The tucunaré, Cichla ocellaris, found throughout tropical South America, is a popular cichlid both in the aquarium and as a game fish.

PHOTO BY HARALD SCHULTZ.

angelfish, that they are hardly recognized as cichlids by fish hobbyists. Still, even the American Cichlid Association, a group that has been in existence since 1967, uses an abstract rendition of an angelfish as its logo, even though there was a certain amount of debate about it at the time since the angel is by no means a typical cichlid body type. Although the discus and angelfish are extreme variations in cichlid body type, there are other specializations that have evolved in the very competitive environs of South America, including the bottom-sifting earth eaters and the very predatory pike cichlids, to mention only a couple. A candidate for the largest cichlid in the world lives in South America, the tucunare, a large predatory form. It competes with the so-called emperor cichlid of Lake Tanganyika, *Boulengerochromis microlepis*, for the largest cichlid of all. It is difficult to tell which is the largest, since individuals vary in size.

While predators have to be large to be able to prey upon smaller fish, the tucunare is not as aggressive and protective of territory as are some smaller cichlids. Cichlids exist in South America that have become what we might call "super cichlids," in that they have maximized the extreme traits of cichlids, such as aggressiveness and versatility. Examples would be the red terror and the green terror, fishes that easily live up to their flamboyant names.

Herichthys festae, the red terror, is being raised in Florida.

PHOTO BY DR. HARRY GRIER COURTESY OF FTFFA.

COMPARISON OF CICHLIDS AROUND THE WORLD

Let us go back and discuss in a little more detail what cichlids are like, in a general sort of way, around the world so that we may be better able to evaluate what South American cichlids have to offer and why so many tropical fish hobbyists are turning to them.

MADAGASCAR

The cichlids of Madagascar certainly have an appeal all of their own, and they represent the most primitive of all the cichlids. Some of them represent almost transitional forms between the ancient marine ancestors which became cichlids and the cichlids themselves. Many of them are

A *Paraetroplus* cichlid from Madagascar.

PHOTO BY MARK SMITH.

quite good looking, and some even lay eggs in a more primitive way, with the eggs strung together in a gelatinous substance, rather than being the adhesive type that can be applied to the surface of a rock, a plant, or even a leaf.

INDIA

The two species of cichlids here seem to be more closely related to the Madagascar cichlids than any other group. Both are extremely

The orange chromide which is found in India, Sri Lanka and some of the ocean waters in between. This is a cichlid.

PHOTO BY DR. HERBERT R. AXELROD.

salt tolerant, and the green chromide spends its adult life in ocean waters, including lagoons. The orange chromide is a popular aquarium fish, as it is colorful, and it is the ideal size for the aquarium. Also, it is not as aggressive as are many cichlids.

AFRICA

Africa has the most species of cichlids, but one of the reasons for that is the great number of endemics (found only there) in the Great Lakes of Africa. Many of the cichlids found throughout the continent greatly resemble the

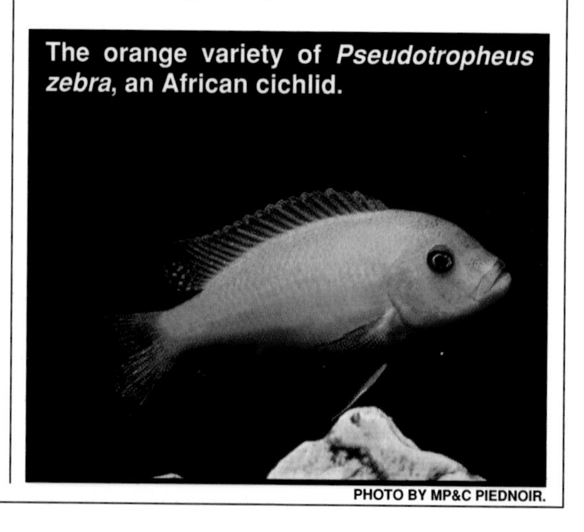

The orange variety of *Pseudotropheus zebra*, an African cichlid.

PHOTO BY MP&C PIEDNOIR.

Pseudotropheus sestonii, an African cichlid.

PHOTO BY EDWARD TAYLOR.

cichlids of the Americas in that many are generalized forms that are quite versatile in habits. A good example of this type is the jewel fish that was long popular with hobbyists before the relatively recent boom in cichlids from the Great Lakes. Each lake has its own type of cichlid group.

LAKE VICTORIA

This has been one of the tragedies for biologists of modern times. This lake is different from the other Rift Lakes in that it is saucer-shaped. It is a large lake, but it is shallow throughout, with lots of plant life growing. The cichlids are all haplochromine (cichlids of the genus *Haplochromis* or derived thereof), and they are all relatively small. Someone got the bright idea of introducing the predatory Nile perch (*Lates niloticus*) into the lake. The cichlids had not evolved with such a large predator and had no defenses against it and no fear of it. For that reason, the Nile perch has proliferated, and the cichlids have been nearly obliterated, many of them without a doubt unknown to science.

The flameback *Haplochromis* from Lake Victoria, Africa.

PHOTO BY MP&C PIEDNOIR.

All of these cichlids are similar in shape but vary in color, and all are mouthbrooding cichlids in which the female incubates the eggs. In this situation, males dig little pits in which the females can place their nonadhesive eggs. The male fertilizes the eggs, and the female picks them up and incubates them until they are free swimming and ready for release. Some species take the young into their mouth, even after release, when danger threatens.

Lates niloticus, the predator introduced into Lake Victoria where it is eating all the open-water *Haplochromis*.

PHOTO BY MP&C PIEDNOIR.

The specializations in the lake have ranged from phytoplankton eaters to snail eaters. With the obliteration of most of the fish, the lake has become overgrown with algae and snails and is a sad reminder of why humankind should resist unnatural relocations of animals.

LAKE MALAWI

This lake has over 200 endemic species, every single one of them a mouthbrooder. One reason for this is that the flock is apparently descended from *Haplochromis*-like ancestors which were already mouthbrooders. There are many variations upon a theme here. Some species only incubate a few eggs, and the young emerge as miniature adults that are fairly good sized. The lake boasts the most colorful cichlids in the world, but they are mostly blue, with occasional reds and oranges. Nonetheless, many of them are quite the equal of many coral reef fishes in coloration.

A colorful African lake cichlid is *Copadichromis borleyi*.

PHOTO BY DR. HERBERT R. AXELROD.

LAKE TANGANYIKA

In this lake, there was a founding diversity of ancestors, so there are mouthbrooders, but there are also substrate spawners. Lacking the spectacular color that is characteristic of Lake Malawi cichlids, several species nonetheless compete in that respect, and there is much more variety in spawning behavior. For that reason, advanced hobbyists have tended to move from Lake Malawi cichlids to those of this lake. But, to be perfectly fair, it must be said that there are those who find the Malawi cichlids endlessly fascinating, and certainly there is still much to learn about them. For whatever reasons, however, the cichlids of Lake Tanganyika are the ones most popular with advanced cichlid hobbyists.

It is interesting to note that, whereas Lake Victoria had few predators in the water, Lake Tanganyika has the Nile perch, an even more spectacular fish predator, the water tiger (*Hydrocynus* species), and six-foot long water cobras, which enter

Tropheus moori, a popular African Lake Tanganyika cichlid.

PHOTO BY MP&C PIEDNOIR.

the water to feed upon fish. And I haven't even mentioned the crocodiles! You get the picture. It is a dangerous lake. Yet cichlids not only survive, they dominate the ichthyofauna.

Spawning methods vary from substrate spawners which spawn in snail shells to mouthbrooders similar to those of Lake Malawi to the emperor cichlid, which spawns in the open and the pair defends its young from all the predatory life in the lake, even biting human divers when they encroach upon their territory.

AMERICAN CICHLIDS

Once again, the cichlids of Central America represent newer species which were able to conquer relatively virgin territory. There has been a certain amount of genetic exchange between some of the cichlids of Central America and South America, especially once the isthmus of Panama was elevated. I am not making a big issue about the differences here. In any case the same type of aquarist who specializes in South American cichlids tends to favor Central American cichlids, too.

What I am trying to explain is the unique appeal of South American cichlids. It is not an easy task, as I was not able to restrain my own enthusiasm for the cichlids of Lake Malawi or Lake Tanganyika. How then to explain the appeal of the relatively drab cichlids of South America? For one thing, of course, they aren't all drab by any means. As just an example, the discus is considered the king of the aquarium world, and the angel is considered the queen. Also, the red terror and green terror may be rough and hard on other fishes, but they are truly beautiful. But I

Regarded by many as the king of the aquarium is the discus, *Symphysodon.*

PHOTO BY DR. HERBERT R. AXELROD.

digress. I am trying to explain the appeal of the South American cichlids and why it is that so many relatively advanced hobbyists are turning to this particular group of cichlids.

Although there is plenty of beauty and exotic form in South American cichlids, the appeal of these cichlids is mainly from their behavior and their diversity. Taking the latter aspect first, South American cichlids range in size from tiny cichlids with the males only reaching slightly over an inch in length to a fish that is a candidate for the largest cichlid in the world. Since cichlids have been in the region for so long, they have probed all possible niches to exploit, and their specialization is especially great. Hence the variation in size, but

This South American favorite dwarf cichlid is *Laetacara curviceps.* Here a female is laying her eggs on a rock.

PHOTO BY HANS JOACHIM RICHTER.

differences also abound in shape and in color.

The behavior involves more than just the exploitation of trophic (feeding) niches. More than from any other region, the cichlids of the Americas work as a team during spawning. Watching a pair cooperate in the care and defense of their young is something of which aquarists and ichthyologists never seem to tire. It is remarkable watching animals, generally considered of such low intelligence, tending their babies and keeping the other partner in sight so that cooperation is possible. Although cichlids in other parts of the world give parental care, it seems to be most highly refined in the cichlids of the New World.

Take just the example of feeding the young from specialized skin secretions. I am not aware of any scientific reports of cichlids from any other part of the world than the Americas exhibiting that behavior. It is most profoundly developed in the discus, in which the body slime is almost an obligatory first food. However, many other species do the same thing as a supplementary source of food, including such rapacious fish as the red terror and the green terror.

Although mouthbrooding of the young seems to be an efficient method of protection, especially in the lake environment, there are only a few mouthbrooding species in which both parents tend the young. The care is left to either the male or the female, with the female usually bearing the burden. That is one of the reasons that substrate spawners are often the preferred fish. Although their method of spawning is more primitive (in the sense that it is an earlier method) than mouthbrooding, substrate spawners have had their share of success, and they have competed well with other cichlids all over the world.

The hobbyist has a choice with the cichlids of South America, as there are mouthbrooding forms in this region, too. In addition, there are many variations on substrate spawning, from laying the eggs in a cave or on a rock in the open to fig leaves as movable platforms. Even flat movable rocks are occasionally used.

Let's take nothing away from African cichlids. They are gorgeous and interesting. But the South American cichlids have something extra to offer. And the reason is that each species has had the time to carve out a niche in very tough and established competition. The results are often stunning. And that is one of the main reasons there has been such a resurgence of interest in South American cichlids.

The earth-eater *Geophagus steindachneri*, a mouth-brooding species. This is a female.

PHOTO BY MP&C PIEDNOIR.

A TANK FOR SOUTH AMERICAN CICHLIDS

A first consideration here is what size cichlids you plan to keep. One of the nice things about South American cichlids is that you have a choice of tiny *Apistogramma* or *Microgeophagus* species, most of which can also be kept in a community tank, or you can keep some small acaras, which are only slightly bigger. None of these acaras should be kept in the typical community tank, however, for they can be quite hard on their fellow fish when they spawn. They are merely trying to drive them away to lessen the danger to their spawn, but the fish can't get away in the home aquarium. You can get still larger fish, such as the green terror or the red terror, but these fish will need a tank of at least a hundred gallons capacity! You can keep a single specimen as a pet, but even it will need a tank of at least forty gallons capacity.

If you don't mind keeping at least a two-hundred-gallon tank, you can tackle the tucunare (*Cichla ocellaris*), but be advised that these fish are determined fish predators, and they are difficult to train to eat anything else. That means that you will need a reliable source of cull guppies or feeder goldfish to keep these animals.

So you have to decide what you are going to keep and then determine the size of the tank. That is not to say that a two hundred-gallon tank filled with the typical community fish and tiny cichlids is not an option. Not only is such a tank beautiful and impressive, but the cichlids will spawn in such a tank without bothering the other residents, other than to chase them out of their area. The point is that some of the larger cichlids need tanks that are quite large. Fortunately, large tanks are available and are relatively inexpensive these days. In the old days, people who kept large cichlids kept them in refrigerator liners or in home made aquariums made of wood with only glass in the front.

A further consideration in the size of the tank you select is whether you want to keep your cichlids for breeding or merely display. The small cichlids can be bred in tanks as small as five gallons in capacity, but the

Breeding discus need a lot of room. This is a 100-gallon tank.

PHOTO BY BERND DEGEN.

disadvantage in such a tank is that the aquarist is unable to view the entire gamut of the fish's behavior. For example, with the *Apistogramma* species (referred to as "apistos" by cichlidophiles), the male must be removed once the eggs are laid. In a larger tank, he would patrol the outer perimeters.

Obviously, if you keep only a pair of cichlids in a tank, it can be smaller than a tank full of big cichlids. A tank of fifty gallons is large enough for spawning all but the biggest of cichlids. In this category would be red terrors, green terrors, oscars, tucunare,

The cubic tank manufactured by Amano in Japan. Amano products are now available in the USA and UK.

PHOTO FROM AMANO'S BOOK *NATURE AQUARIUM WORLD.*

Golden rams in a cubic tank designed, manufactured and photographed by Takashi Amano, from his book *NATURE AQUARIUM WORLD.*

Takashi Amano designed, manufactured and installed this huge aquarium just for cichlids.

PHOTO BY TAKASHI AMANO FROM HIS BOOK *NATURE AQUARIUM WORLD*.

as all of these fish would need a spawning tank larger than fifty gallons. Except for the tucunare, a hundred-gallon tank should be large enough to house a spawning pair.

species which are somewhat larger and more formidable. However, it is possible that both of these species can be kept in a community tank and even spawn without harming the other

Community tanks set up in a restaurant.

PHOTO BY TAKASHI AMANO FROM HIS BOOK *NATURE AQUARIUM WORLD*.

residents. They simply keep them out of their area.

COMMUNITY TANKS

When we speak of the typical community tanks, we mean the tanks that house a variety of small and colorful fish. Usually these consist of guppies, platies, small tetras, and tiny catfish, such as *Corydoras* species. Some cichlids are small and can be trusted, even when in a spawning mood, not to kill their fellow aquarium denizens. These would include the ram and some of the *Apistogramma* species. Keyhole cichlids and the blue acara are two South American cichlid

In this case, the term "area" needs definition. You see, with either of these species, spawning is initiated by the fish pairing up. They then begin cleaning a surface for the eggs. If they have the option, that area will be inside a cave of some sort. For example, if you place a flowerpot on its side in the tank (or upside down with notches in the sides), it is almost inevitable that it will be selected as the spawning site. Once the eggs are laid and fertilized, the pair will take turns fanning the eggs, while the other one guards the area. At this stage, the area is about six inches to a foot from the site where the eggs were laid. In about four days, the eggs hatch, and they are transferred to a pit in the gravel. Almost without fail, several pits are dug, and the young are transferred regularly from one pit to another. It was once thought that this was done to confuse possible predators as to where the young were. A more compelling explanation is that the baby fish are transferred in order to insure that they are cleaned of debris in the process, since the parents transfer the young in their mouths. (The cleaning helps keep the young free of disease-causing bacteria and fungi.) The territory of the fish is slightly expanded at this stage, since there are the spawning pits to accommodate, too. And the area around the territory that fish are excluded from continues to be about six inches to a foot from the fry, but the parental fish become more aggressive at this stage, and the area can be expanded somewhat.

Once the fry are free swimming, things change dramatically, as the territory the fish define and defend now begins to move with the fry, and the boundaries are expanded dramatically. In most species, the territory is the entire tank. In the case of the blue acara and the keyhole cichlids, the territory is usually relatively small, and that is the reason that they can spawn in a large community tank without maiming or killing their tank-mates.

This tank is 6 feet long and made to order for dwarf cichlids.

PHOTO BY TAKASHI AMANO FROM HIS BOOK *NATURE AQUARIUM WORLD.*

Of course, a community tank of small fish is not the only type of community tank that exists. It is also possible to have a community tank of cichlids. In such tanks, the size of the fish, as well as the aggression levels, must be carefully matched. If a species spawns, they will be the dominant ones in the tank. A tricky situation is when two pairs spawn simultaneously. You can bet that they spawned at opposite ends of the tank, and there will be trouble brewing once the territories of both species begin to expand!

Even with the problems just discussed, community cichlid tanks are quite practical for most people, and they are probably the most popular way to keep cichlids. Even in these tanks, many hobbyists keep some other species of fish that tend to dwell in the upper regions of the tank. After all, South American cichlids live with other fish in nature, and, for the most part, they tend to ignore them, other than to keep them away when they are spawning. Depending on the size of the cichlids involved, different species are used, from jewel tetras to silver dollars. The important point here is to have fish that are fast swimmers, so that they can evade the cichlids when they decide to make a pass at them. The reason for keeping these non-cichlid species is that the random swimming of other fish species tends to make the cichlids more at ease and to be out in the open more. Cichlid behavior is generally of the measured type, with a lot of lurking, hiding, and posturing. But they seem to feel more at home when there are other species of fish in constant motion. Such species are often used even in breeding tanks, and they are called "dither fish" in such cases.

Obviously, the size of your tank is going to depend on how many cichlids you want to keep and what size they will be. A large tank of cichlids can be a spectacular sight. Fortunately, aquaria are better constructed and of a more reasonable price than they have ever been. For that reason, it is possible to purchase several young cichlids. Start saving your pennies for a two-hundred or even a five-hundred-gallon tank a couple of years down the road.

For people who want a really large tank, the temptation is always to custom build such a tank. I have seen a few beautifully made tanks of great size. These were, almost without exception, tanks made by people experienced in cabinet making, and the giant tanks were made of wood, with heavy plate glass in the front only. Such tanks were waterproofed on the inside with fiber glass resin, and they were sometimes reinforced by the actual use of fiber glass itself. Although I am generally in favor of purchasing commercially-built tanks, I can attest to the durability of a properly constructed wooden tank, as I still have one that was made by a cabinet-maker hobbyist many years ago. In fact, he is long dead, but his handwork still graces my study.

Another consideration is managing the aggression in a cichlid tank. Turning to a particular tank in my memory which was kept by a master aquarist, it was filled with an abundance of petrified wood and other rockwork. The bottom covering was a mixture of fine and coarse sand. Of course, petrified wood is difficult to come by these days, but a variety of rocks can be utilized. Please be aware that some rocks can leach out minerals or toxins which can be harmful to the fish. Rocks of strictly volcanic origin are usually the best to use. As a matter of fact, pumice is particularly good because it is light and it can be easily shaped with a tool to fit within the contours of the tank and to provide caves for the fish.

If you don't want to select your own rock, there are commercially sold artificial rocks that have two main advantages. They are appealing in appearance, and they are hollow and, for that reason, are easy to handle. That is no small consideration, for the chances are that when you want to move a particular fish, you will have to remove all the rockwork, as cichlids are masters of the maze that rockwork creates, and they can be downright impossible to catch as long as it is in the tank.

Some plants can be kept in the tank, as a friend of mine, as just one example, kept a tough and tall species of *Vallisneria* growing in the back, protected by his make-shift rockwork. But most cichlidophiles do without and avoid the hassle. The most they keep are floating plants, such as water sprite, duckweed, or anacharis. Duckweed is particularly popular because it provides a covering to diffuse the light, providing a nice cast to the tank. It also multiplies rapidly, and it provides supplementary food for those cichlids inclined to take it. In fact, it also harbors small crustaceans that the cichlids may also eat in addition to (or instead of) the duckweed.

An excellent cichlid tank which contains only sand and rocks...and cichlids which can dig to their heart's content. The cichlids shown here are all African species.

PHOTO BY DOSHIN KOBAYASHI.

Filtration can be as simple as a few inside filters or as complex as a series of compound filters, including such exotic ones as algae filters and trickle filters. Most cichlidophiles who keep South American cichlids make use of either inside box or foam filters—especially is this true if

Cichlids enjoy duckweed. It floats, is a suitable addition to their diet, and is never in the way of spawning rituals.

the hobbyists are trying to breed cichlids. The filters are changed frequently, and so is the water. Also, good aquarium practices are followed in managing the water. For that reason, someone with the simplest of systems can outdo a more careless aquarist with exotic filtration.

Nevertheless, hobbyists who simply want to keep a community tank of South American cichlids will very likely want to make use of some of the more complicated filter systems. For that reason, I thought that I would give you a quick overview of what is available.

A rock aquarium that was set up for African cichlids but could be used for digging, plant-disturbing South American cichlids as well.

FILTRATION

There are two aspects to water filtration. One is to clear the water of debris. The other is to break down the metabolites that are excreted by the fish. The first makes the water look good, and the second keeps the water livable for the fish. Water can be kept in good shape by frequent partial water changes. That is one reason for keeping fish that prosper in the water provided by your local municipality. You don't have to worry about modifying any of the water that you use for your partial water changes. Fortunately, most South American cichlids prosper in soft water, and they can adapt to even hard water. Most of them can even spawn in hard water with no apparent ill effects on the young. Only discus, rams, and some of the *Apistogramma* species require soft water with a relatively low pH, but more about that later.

If you have decided to go ahead and modify your water

PHOTO BY DOSHIN KOBAYASHI.

because you just have to keep some species that doesn't do well in your water, it is more important than ever to have biological filtration. Such filtration is so called because it involves the use of various different types of bacteria for breaking ammonia down into nitrite and yet another group of bacteria for breaking the nitrite down into nitrate. The most famous biological filter is the one that has been the workhorse filter for many decades now, the undergravel filter.

The problem is that many South American cichlids can cause a problem with undergravel filters. Although it may not happen often, even the smallest South American cichlids can dig holes clear down to the filter plate of the undergravel filter. This completely compromises the filter efficiency, as the least resistance for the water is to go down through the filter plate where there is no gravel. The object of the undergravel filter is to pass the water through the gravel. In time, the proper types of bacteria colonize the outside of each gravel particle. So the biological filter is attained. Mechanical filtration is provided, too, as the undergravel filter will pull all the debris into the gravel. An undergravel filter will keep a tank about as clear as any filter.

As with nearly all things in life, there are drawbacks to the undergravel filter. I have already mentioned the one regarding cichlids. They will often dig holes down to the filter plate. Fortunately, this problem can be circumvented in a couple of ways. First, a layer of gravel can be placed on the filter plate. Then plastic screening is placed over that layer. More gravel is placed over the screening. That way the cichlids can't dig down past the screening, so the filter is always functioning.

Another approach is to place down a layer of gravel, but place a thin sponge mat over it and then grating that has been cut to fit the tank. The type of grating that is used to diffuse large fluorescent lights is perfect. A second layer of gravel is placed over the grating. Try to make it high enough above the grating that the cichlids can dig a hole deep enough for a spawning pit, but the grating will keep them from digging any deeper.

Another problem with the undergravel filter is that debris tends to accumulate in the gravel in the tank so fast that the bacteria are unable to break it down fast enough to keep up with it. This accumulation of organic matter creates dead spots in which almost no water is going through, because it is being channeled through areas that are not blocked. One way to circumvent this problem is to vacuum the gravel on a regular basis. This can be done with a siphon tube equipped with a special adaptor. That way you can vacuum the gravel of debris when you make your partial water changes. However, there are also powered vacuum devices, with a vacuum bag, too, that enable you to vacuum easily and on a daily basis.

Another approach is to use a reverse-flow undergravel filter. This involves running the water down what would normally be the lift tubes and passing the water up through the gravel. An important point here is that the water is filtered before being sent down beneath the gravel. The object here is to keep the particulate matter separate from the biological filter. That way the gravel tends to stay clear of debris almost indefinitely. Since cichlids tend to be fairly large, the gravel should still be vacuumed regularly, but it doesn't have to be quite as religious a practice as it does with the common undergravel filter.

Of course, the undergravel filter is not the only biological filter. There are others, but they are all strictly biological; they won't double as mechanical filters, too, as is the case with the old standby undergravel filter. But some of them are even more efficient biological filters than the undergravel device. So you may want to consider one of these, particularly if you are keeping fish species for which you have to alter the pH and hardness of the water. For if you use one or more of these devices, you won't have to make as many partial water changes.

One such device is the trickle filter. These filters are also known as wet/dry filtration. This is the system which had everyone so excited just a few years ago. Results were spectacular compared with what we had experienced before. The filter is strictly a biological filter, so the water should be pre-filtered for this device. Most of the commercial wet/dry filters have a prefilter built into the intake, even if it is only a sponge filter. (I say "only," but actually sponge filters are quite effective *if they are cleaned on a regular and frequent basis*. Cleaning should consist of scrubbing and rinsing the sponge in some aquarium water which has been siphoned out for the purpose. The reason for using the aquarium water is to preserve the bacteria which will inhabit a sponge filter and provide some biological filtration. Naturally, no detergent or soap should be utilized in the cleaning. The sponge should then be replaced and the aquarium water discarded.

further purpose was to increase the exchange of gases so that ammonia could be dissipated and oxygen increased.

The dry part of the filter, then, consists of a tray of inert porous material, such as clay granules, and a spray bar which wets the material evenly with water from the tank. A dry filter can be suspended above the tank, and

Many cichlids dig up the gravel either in search of food or preparatory to spawning. (*Biotodoma cupido* is shown).

The reason wet/dry filters are often referred to as "trickle" filters is that not many commercial models have incorporated the wet part of the wet/dry filtration, or, at least, it is only a small part of the filter. The idea was to improve upon the undergravel filter by maximizing the amount of oxygen exposure to the bacteria so that it would function more efficiently. A

the water simply trickles over the medium, and the shallow flow of the water allows for good gas exchange. The bacteria function up to 20 times as efficiently when utilized in this manner. Of course, there is no wet part to such a filter; nevertheless, devices just described are quite popular.

Another approach is to use what is commonly called a tower,

and this has been the most common method of the commercial wet/dry filters. The medium for "housing" the bacteria is what are commonly called "bio-balls." These are plastic spheres with as many surfaces as possible for the desirable bacteria. A drip plate or spray bar is placed over the tower, and the water is taken from the aquarium and run through the tower at not too fast a rate. This again provides the exposure to the air that is desirable. The only problem is that a tower is enclosed, so the air can become stagnant. For that reason, a flow of air is pumped upward (counter to the flow of water) or openings in the tower are provided for ventilation.

Another medium utilized in a tower is coiled plastic matting. This material has lots of air spaces, so it satisfies the requirement for the water's being exposed to lots of air for a good exchange of gases. Almost always a rotating spray bar is utilized in a tower with coiled matting, as the roundness of the matting is matched by the circular distribution of water by the spray bar. The spray bar is turned by the force of the water itself, as the holes are placed strategically so that the water leaving the spray bar imparts motion to it, much like many garden hose sprinklers.

The idea behind the wet portion of the filter is to utilize anaerobic, or non-oxygen using, bacteria for breaking down nitrates. At its simplest, such a filter consists of an inert medium, preferably porous, and the chamber should be kept dark (to avoid competition from algae), and there should be a low water turnover. The last requirement is what has made it difficult to incorporate the wet portion of the wet/dry filter with the dry trickle filter. The movement of water through the dry system is too fast for the movement of water through the wet section. Compromises are made, and many manufacturers include a wet section in the sump of the trickle filter. The sump is of fairly good size in these cases, and that gives the water time to "sit" while waiting for the sump pump to return the water to the aquarium. This allows the anaerobic bacteria to at least have some time for breaking down nitrates. The problem is that the water entering the sump is very well oxygenated. One way for getting around this problem is to have a very deep medium so that the bacteria can thrive at the bottom. Still, the wet portion of the filter generally seems to function better separately, and de-nitrators have been invented that actually work. Although trickle filters are still in a process of development, I must confess that few cichlid people use them. Again, it would be most desirable if you are keeping fish that need water different from your tap water. Even so, there is a biological filter that is simpler and more compact. It can be used by itself or in conjunction with your trickle filter.

The name is imposing: *fluidized bed biological filtration*! This is a relatively new system, but everything that I have experienced and all my discussions with people and all my readings indicate that this new system is an efficient biological filter. It consists of a bed of relatively small gravel which is kept in a state of constant movement, with a good portion of it being suspended in the water. There is a built-in pump which directs a spray or sprays of water at a strategic point or points, and the filter medium (usually fine beach sand) is contained in a holder shaped like an upside-down pyramid. (Some recent designs involve utilizing a cylindrical shape. In fact, the first time I saw one, I thought that it was a new type of protein skimmer, at first glance.) If nothing else, fluidized biological filters are fun to watch. While not actually new, it has taken some time for these types of filters to be properly sized and adapted to the home aquarium.

Apistogramma agassizi.

PHOTO BY HANS JOACHIM RICHTER.

One of the main points of this device is that all of the filter medium is utilized and is active in the process of biological filtration. (It is worth noting here that, of course, the gravel merely provides a "home" for the beneficial bacteria. What this filter does is provide the bacteria equal exposure to any nutrients available.) An important point here is that "dead spots" are virtually non-existent and that the fluidized bed biological filters seems to need virtually no maintenance.

These filters are currently being manufactured to draw water from the sump of the wet/dry filter or from the return tube of a canister filter. (Many hobbyists who are completely sold on the fluidized bed filtration use it in place of trickle filtration.) The water should be filtered before being introduced to the fluidized filter. This filter functions only as a biological filter, not a mechanical one. But its biological filtering powers are excellent.

One of the most significant problems with any conventional biological filter is that the layers of bacteria that accumulate on the surface of the media can get quite thick, thereby blocking the transfer of nutrients and oxygen to the lower layers. In time, this results in a mature and thick colony of bacteria that consume fewer nutrients than a younger, thinner culture. Because of the constant movement of the medium, there is a constant sloughing of older layers of bacteria which ensures that thick layers are avoided and that those present are the thinner more efficient converters.

Fluidized bed biological filters have more surface area than any other type of biological filter. Because of this, they can be compactly designed. There is virtually no maintenance involved. In short, these fluidized filters can handle just about anything. They do more work, cost less, and require less maintenance than all other biological filters.

Water may be introduced into one of these filters by two methods. You can utilize a small powerhead from the sump in your wet/dry filter or you may add a T-fitting into the return line from your main pump and divert part of the water flow to the inlet valve, using the attached valve to regulate the flow into the filter. (There is a limit to the amount of water which can be processed through the filter.) Finally, fluidized bed filters have become sufficiently popular that they are manufactured with their own pumps and pre-filters. These are the models that most cichlidophiles have been using. They simply hang on the back or side of the tank. Cichdophiles who use one filter for a bank of tanks have access to fluidized bed filters that are big and built for just that purpose. That is, there are fluidized bed biological filters which are manufactured to function as centralized filters for a series of tanks. These often have their own pumps for moving the water to the tanks, and needless to say, they are quite large. Of course, the use of such filters is going to be pretty much restricted to the very serious hobbyist who is primarily interested in breeding different species of cichlids.

Another biological filter that is worth knowing about even if you don't use it is the algae filter or algae "scrubber." Algae scrubbers are often called *algal turf scrubbers*, and these devices have their adherents. The scrubbers are basically shallow troughs with a plastic mesh screen. Water is often pumped to the troughs by means of a "dump bucket" to simulate waves. The waves help the algae exchange gases, through exposure to the air in between surges. The various turf-forming algae which grow on the screens remove ammonia, nitrate, phosphate, and heavy metals from the water. The screens have to be periodically serviced by removing them and scraping off the excess algal growth with a plastic scraper.

Of course, the troughs are under intense lighting. One of the problems has been to design systems which fit well on home aquaria, as the system was first developed and utilized by Dr. Walter Adey at the Smithsonian Museum's Natural History Museum in Washington. Hang-on models which fit on the back of an aquarium are available, as are large units which can service a number of aquaria. Molded

Symphysodon discus discus.

COLLECTED AND PHOTOGRAPHED BY DR. HERBERT R. AXELROD.

models are now available that can fit any size system. They can be installed above, behind, or below tanks.

It is interesting to note that very few people are ambivalent about algae scrubbers. Hobbyists either love them or hate them. They have been mostly used by marine hobbyists and many of them have had good success with them. Very few of even the most ardent turf scrubber advocates are in favor of using the algae scrubbers as the sole method of treating the water. While the algae scrubbers do a good job of removing various undesirable substances, they also release dissolved organic compounds into the water which can turn the water a yellowish cast. This problem can be remedied by placing bags of a high-quality grade of activated carbon in the aquarium.

Generally speaking, cichlid people are direct, and they prefer systems that are as simple as possible, but I wanted you to know about the latest in technology. Most of you will use an undergravel filter or an outside mechanical filter (or inside mechanical filters) and make frequent partial water changes.

As for changing the water, it all depends on which way you are going. The easiest is if you have soft water and you want to keep hard water fishes. All you have to do then is to buy salts that contain the minerals for reproducing such water. They are sold commercially in fish stores. Just follow the directions on the package. (But I should emphasize here that very few South American cichlids require hard water. Most prefer neutral to soft water.)

With hard water going to soft, it is a tougher proposition, but one method is to utilize peat moss in the filters. If possible, get to know some killifish people in your area, as they are the masters of the alchemy of peat moss. Killifish people simply dump peat moss onto the bottom of their tanks (after boiling it and processing it), because they don't have to worry about the tiny amounts of excrement their tiny fish will put out. This would be true to some extent with the tiniest of South American cichlids. But most South American cichlids are too big to ignore in that respect, and besides, the cichlids are going to be around for a lot longer than the killies, which are basically short lived animals. So the peat moss can be placed in a layer in the undergravel filter or it can be placed in an inside filter. Killifish people will tell you how it should be boiled and soaked in water many times before actually being used. Many claims are made for peat moss, from softening the water to adding desirable hormones. There is much folklore to this material, and it can be difficult to separate the whimsy from the whamsy, but it has a large following among aquarists, and it must be admitted that the keeping of fish is as much an art as a science.

A more scientific, if more expensive, approach is to utilize a reverse osmosis device. These devices produce water that is completely pure of minerals, organic compounds, or metals. In cichlids, as they are nearly all capable of adapting to hard water, and most inhabit areas in which the water is soft to medium. So

Old favorites like the severum, *Heros severus*, are bred commercially in great number; tank-bred specimens usually are very adaptable to a wide range of water hardnesses as long as changes are not made abruptly.

PHOTO BY H. J. RICHTER.

fact, the water must be mixed with at least some of your tap water, for it is simply too soft for any fish.

The final alternative is to buy bottled water that is of the hardness and pH that you want. By now, you are beginning to understand why I recommend matching the fish to the water, rather than the other way around! In any case, we don't really have to worry about providing soft water for our South American why did I tell you about making water soft? Because cichlid people have the reputation of being much smarter than other fish people, and I am fulfilling my part in maintaining that image by educating readers as completely as possible!

FURTHER COMMENTS ABOUT THE CICHLID AQUARIUM

There are a hundred ways to fix up a cichlid aquarium, far more than I can cover here. Cichlid people are ingenious. I have known cichlid people who built their own aquaria from wood, with glass only in the front. Some of the tanks were absolutely gigantic, and some were so well crafted and finished that they made a nice addition to any house. (And some were so huge that they would have qualified as a full-scale addition to the house!) Others didn't look so good, but they were serviceable, and they were only kept in the garage or fish room anyway.

Furnishings have ranged from exotic rockwork to cinder blocks to PVC piping of all different sizes. Obviously, the latter didn't look as good, but the fish liked it just as much! The main idea is to provide the fish with caves and demarcations of territory. In the wild, the fish do some things that we can't provide for in our tanks. For example, some dig a complex system of tunnels in the substrate of their natural habitat. Fortunately, they will adapt to the furnishings we provide them. One of the most surprising things about cichlids is that most of them will spawn in captivity. That they do so is a sign of their versatility and adaptability.

The oscar, *Astronotus ocellatus*, is a South American species, but the red variety shown here was developed in Thailand.

PHOTO BY DR. HERBERT R. AXELROD.

Finally, all types of persons are drawn to cichlids, from university professors to physicians to garage mechanics. (And, of course, that is not counting professional ichthyologists!) Each type sees different things in the animals, perhaps, but they all swap the same stories and share information and camaraderie. You would think that the university types would have the most success. Sometimes they do, but just as often, it is the garage mechanic who spawns the most difficult fish and keeps his animals the best. While there is much science to cichlid keeping, it still remains very much an art. And cichlids seem to be one of those rare bridges between intellectuals and blue collar workers, with physicians, as an example, taking tips from plumbers on how to provide the proper conditions for a given species of cichlid. Aggressive as so many of them are, it is ironic how cichlids provide a common bond of friendship for so many people.

CICHLIDS FOR THE COMMUNITY TANK

In this case we are talking about the typical community tank. We are considering cichlids (South Americans only, of course!) that can be safely kept in a typical community tank with the usual small fish that are kept in such tanks, without their doing harm to tankmates. In most cases, it is because the cichlids are small. In a couple of cases, it is simply because they are quite gentle and not nearly so territorial as their brethren of the family Cichlidae.

I will list these in alphabetical order by scientific name. Although I will also utilize the popular name when there is one available, it is important that the reader understand something about scientific names. First, don't worry about pronunciation. People all over the world, including scientists, pronounce the words differently. Even within a country, the names are pronounced differently. It wasn't always thus. There was a time when there were strict rules for pronunciation, and diacritical markings helped as a guide to pronunciation. But even then scientists around the world pronounced the words differently, as they were influenced by their own language. Finally, it was decided that pronunciation wasn't that important, and the diacritical markings were eliminated.

A few general guidelines may be helpful so that everyone approximates the same pronunciation. The words are generally Latin, and since the language is no longer spoken, no one is certain about the exact pronunciation of all the words. Anyway, the words are occasionally Greek, so that situation muddies the waters, too. The names that there is really no reason to mispronounce are the patronyms. These are designations that are given a fish in order to honor a person. If the person is a male, the name ends in "i," and if the person is a female, it ends in "ae"; "i" is pronounced like the letter, but if there are two "i"s after the name, the first "i" is pronounced "ee." For example, *smithi* would simply be pronounced "smith-EYE." If it were *smithii*, it would be pronounced "smith-ee-EYE." Similarly, *trewavasae* would be pronounced "trewavas-EE." The "ae" and "i" endings follow Latin rules of gender, but they are handy because they let us know something about the gender of the person being honored, too.

Please note that scientific names are put in italics or underlined to set them off as coming from a foreign language. Also, note that the first name, the generic name, is capitalized, while the second, the species name, is not. Thus, the scientific name for humankind is *Homo sapiens*. The generic name is normally a noun, and the species name is an adjective. (Like *casa blanca* in Spanish means white house, but with the adjective following the noun.) In our name, *Homo sapiens*, the meaning is "humankind wise" or "wise humankind." One value of devising a naming system is that we get to give ourselves a good name! Incidentally, now that you know about the name for our species being properly written as *Homo sapiens*, you will notice that newspapers misuse it all the time, failing to use italics or to capitalize the generic name.

The value of scientific names is that they are used throughout the world by scientists and by anyone else with a particular interest in the living things under study. So we are more likely to know what animal we are discussing than we are with popular names, which tend to vary within the same country, and they certainly vary throughout the world. Besides that, scientific names show relationships. For example, if you were to see the name *Homo erectus* or *Homo neanderthalus*, you would know that they are supposed to be related to *Homo sapiens*—at least close enough to be within the same genus.

In the case of fish, you know that *Pterophyllum scalare* and *Pterophyllum altum* are closely related because they have the same generic name. The same would be true with *Apistogramma cacatuoides* and *Apistogramma bitaeniata*.

Although scientific names are universal, they are not immutable. Additional research or new information can result in a refinement of our knowledge, and that can result in some name changes. In fact, some of the generic names have been changed in many of the South American species. For example, *Microgeophagus ramirezi*, the ram, was once known as *Apistogramma ramirezi*, but further study revealed that the ram was sufficiently different anatomically and in behavior to need a different genus. This is universally accepted among ichthyologists, so we have the species listed under the new names. In some cases, such new names have not been accepted by the entire scientific community, and so I am using the old names and just mentioning the proposed new names. That way, you will know what fish is being discussed in older literature. The guide for determining how to list each species, though, is how the animal is being listed in current scientific literature. (Researchers are conservative and slow to change long-held names.)

Okay, then, here are some species that can be kept in community tanks, with a little information about each one of them. When there is no popular name listed, it simply means that one has not been invented. This is either because the fish never became very popular or because advanced aquarists primarily kept the fish and were simply at ease with the scientific name.

A pair of *Apistogramma agassizi* spawning. The eggs are hanging from the roof of the rocky cave. The female, the lighter of the two fish, has her ovipositor extended.

PHOTO BY HANS JOACHIM RICHTER.

Scientific name: ***Apistogramma agassizi***
Popular name: **Spade Tail Apisto**

This fish was described scientifically in 1875, and it occurs throughout the Amazon, right up to the base of the Andes Mountains. This is a species that has been a staple in the tropical fish hobby among those who like small cichlids. All the known *Apistogramma* species spawn in a very similar way. The female turns a yellow coloration and guards the eggs by herself and takes primary care of the young, with the male patrolling the perimeter. Even during a spawning, the fish are unlikely to harm other inhabitants, as these are such mild fish that even a female guppy may challenge the fry-guarding female. In nature, most of the *Apistogramma* species are harem spawners, with one male presiding over the territory of several females, so it may be best to keep one male with several females in a community tank.

All apistos are found in especially soft water in the wild, but I have successfully spawned many species in San Diego water, which is close to liquid rock, so obviously they are versatile. Still, I may have been quite fortunate, and the reader is advised to provide soft water for spawning at least. But there is no question that *Apistogramma* species can prosper in hard water if you aren't worried about breeding them.

In most of the apisto species, the male reaches about three

This sequence of eight photos shows the male and female *Apistogramma agassizi*, courting, selecting a spawning site and then cleaning the spawning site.

PHOTOS BY HANS JOACHIM RICHTER.

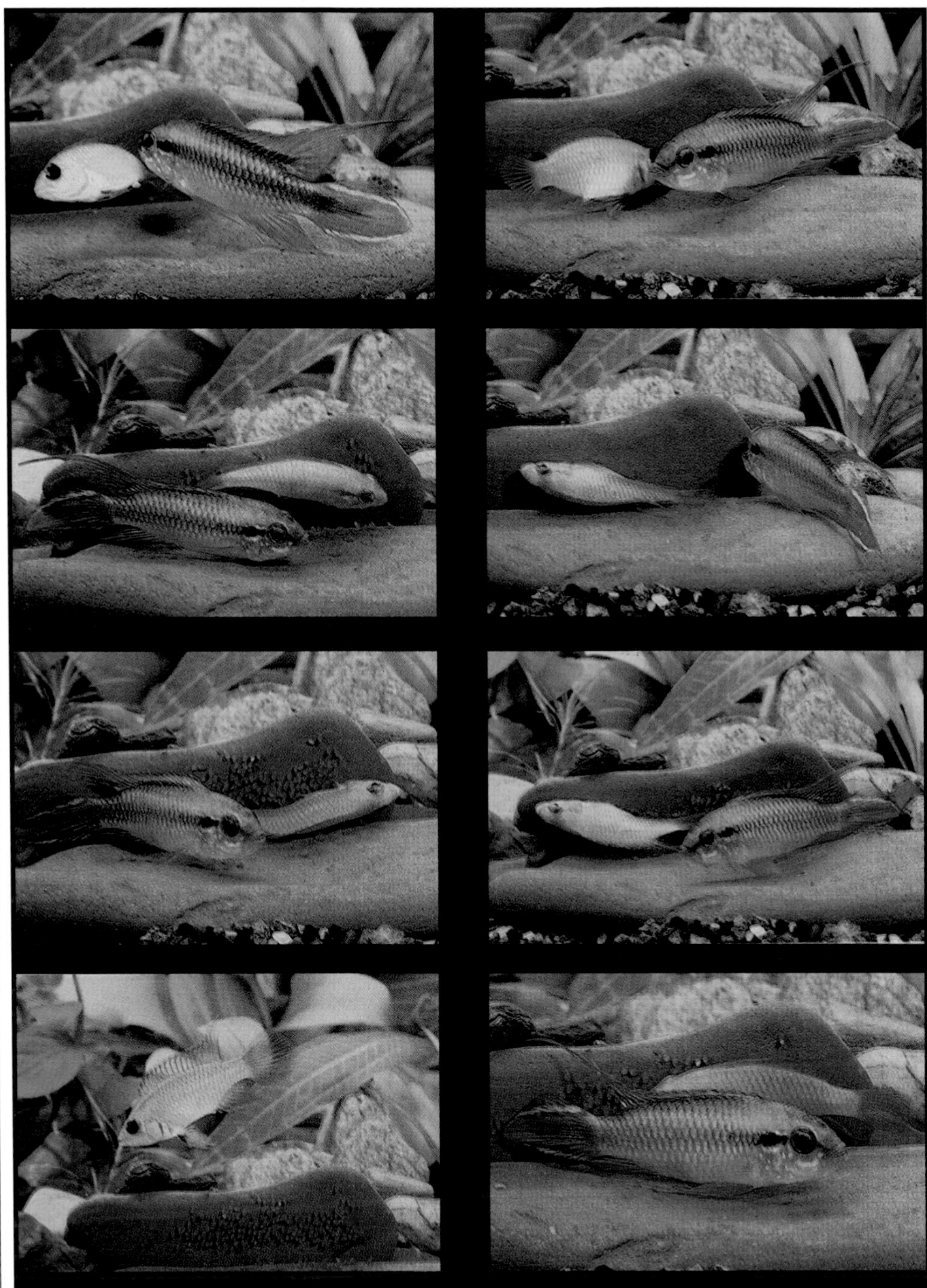

This sequence of eight photos shows the *Apistogramma agassizi* preparing to spawn, actually spawning and guarding their red eggs.

PHOTOS BY HANS JOACHIM RICHTER.

inches in length, with the female reaching about an inch to two inches. They spawn at a much smaller size. The apistos are short lived for cichlids, only living for about three to four years. There are a great many species of them, but most of them are relatively colorless and only appreciated by the real apisto devotee. In any case, I'll list just a few here.

In spite of the fact that these fish are small, the young are able to take newly-hatched brine shrimp once they are free swimming.

Scientific name: ***Apistogramma bitaeniata***

Although this is a popular fish, there is no popular name for it, but it has gone by many synonyms. There was a time that all the apisto species that had the extended dorsal rays were known as *Apistogramma* U_1 or U_2 or U_3, including even one U_4. The "u" stood for "unbekannt," the German for "unknown," as the genus was recognized but the species was not known. This was back before the U2 spy planes became famous! Then this species was described by Meinken as *Apistogramma kleei*, and the species was known for a while in the hobby under that name. As it turned out, Meinken had not been able to review all the preserved material, as the species had been described as *Apistogramma bitaeniata* in 1936, and that name

Apistogramma bitaeniata.

PHOTO BY R. SCHREIBER.

A pair of *Apistogramma bitaeniata* spawning on a stone.

PHOTO BY HANS JOACHIM RICHTER.

took precedence. (The earliest name used in a valid scientific description is the one that has priority according to biological convention.)

Scientific name: ***Apistogramma borellii***

One reason that there are two "i"s at the end of the species name is that the species was described in 1906, and it was named in honor of Dr. A. Borelli, who discovered the species. It has a wide distribution in the Mato Grosso and almost every river which connects with it.

This fish is known for its large fins, and it was once known incorrectly in the hobby as *Apistogramma reitzigi*, and it may be found in the older hobby literature under that name.

Another variety of *Apistogramma bitaeniata*.

PHOTO BY J. VIERKE.

A spawning sequence of *Apistogramma borelli*.

PHOTOS BY HANS JOACHIM RICHTER.

The spawning setup used for breeding *Apistogramma borelli.*

PHOTO BY HANS JOACHIM RICHTER.

Apistogramma cacatuoides.

PHOTO BY MP&C PIEDNOIR.

Scientific name: ***Apistogramma cacatuoides***

This is another one of those fish that was once known as *Apistogramma* U_2. It was described in 1951, and it is found in the upper Solimoes to Colombia and Peru. It is hard to believe now, but it was once confused in the hobby with *Apistogramma bitaeniata.* The coloration is quite different in this species, and the body shape is considerably more stocky. And I should point out that there is a variation of coloration in nearly all the apisto species. Most species have such a wide geographical range that some individual groups get cut off and develop slight differences in coloration over the eons.

Scientific name: ***Apistogramma nijsseni***

This fish has created some excitement because of the

Apistogramma cacatuoides spawning.

PHOTO BY J. VIERKE.

PHOTO BY P. DE RHAM.

Apistogramma nijsseni female.

Apistogramma nijsseni male.

PHOTO BY MP&C PIEDNOIR.

unusual color pattern of the female when breeding. Normally, spawning females turn yellow, with a stripe through the eye and maybe one spot on the sides.

Scientific name: ***Apistogramma trifasciata***

Just in case the reader has not guessed, I have a special spot in my heart for the apistos that have elongated dorsal fins and this is one of those species. And I should also warn the reader that my personal tastes don't favor apistos, but that is probably because I was imprinted early on large and rough cichlids! (And yet, I fully appreciate *Microgeophagus ramirezi*!)

Scientific name: ***Cleithracara maronii***
Popular name: **Keyhole Cichlid**

This fish was first described as *Acara maronii* in 1882, and it is

Apistogramma trifasciata, a male not in breeding colors.

PHOTO BY MP&C PIEDNOIR.

The spawning setup for *Apistogramma trifasciata.*

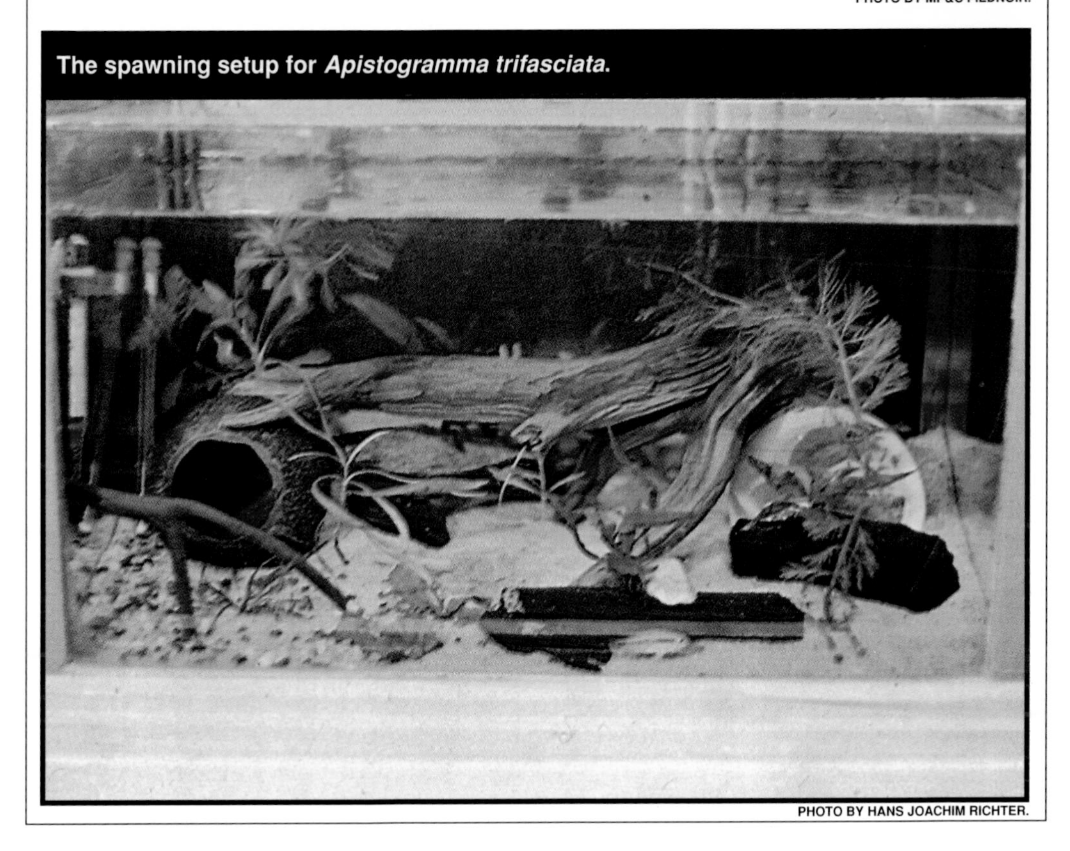

PHOTO BY HANS JOACHIM RICHTER.

Microgeophagus ramirezi, the wild color form.

PHOTO BY RUDA ZUKAL.

found in the Guianas. It reaches a length of about four inches, but it is one of the most gentle of all cichlids. The parents share the care of the young, but they are quite gentle in their protection. They should not be kept with cichlids other than the ones listed in this chapter, as they are so gentle (and I do appreciate *them*!). The fish will be found in the older literature as *Aequidens maronii.*

Cleithacara maronii.

PHOTO BY MP&C PIEDNOIR.

Scientific name: ***Microgeophagus ramirezi***
Popular name: **Ram**

This fish was named after the collector, Manuel Vicente Ramirez. Since Americans butchered the scientific name, the popular name of "ram" somehow came about. There is also a golden variety, but, as so often is the case, the wild color is the most beautiful. Although the colors are somewhat subdued, the fish is truly beautiful when in full coloration, and its appearance has a real touch of class.

In spawning, both parents clean off a rock and both of them care for the young, just like some of the large cichlids. However, they are only about two inches long, at the maximum, and they are quite gentle, so they are no threat to the other members of a community tank. They will be one of your favorite additions to the tank. Although I spawned the species in our hard San Diego water, I had the best success in water that had been softened.

Scientific name: ***Nannacara anomala***

This species is very similar to *Apistogramma* species in behavior, but it is considerably different anatomically. I called them "animated watermelons" when I first saw them. They look merely transparent brown under bright light. But when they are in good condition and the lighting is not too bright, the male has a bluish iridescence to him. These fish spawn in an identical manner to apistos, except the female does not turn yellow. Once again, this is a species which can spawn in a community tank without terrorizing and killing the other inhabitants, although they will be chased from the spawning area.

The golden form of the ramirezi.

PHOTO BY DR. HERBERT R. AXELROD

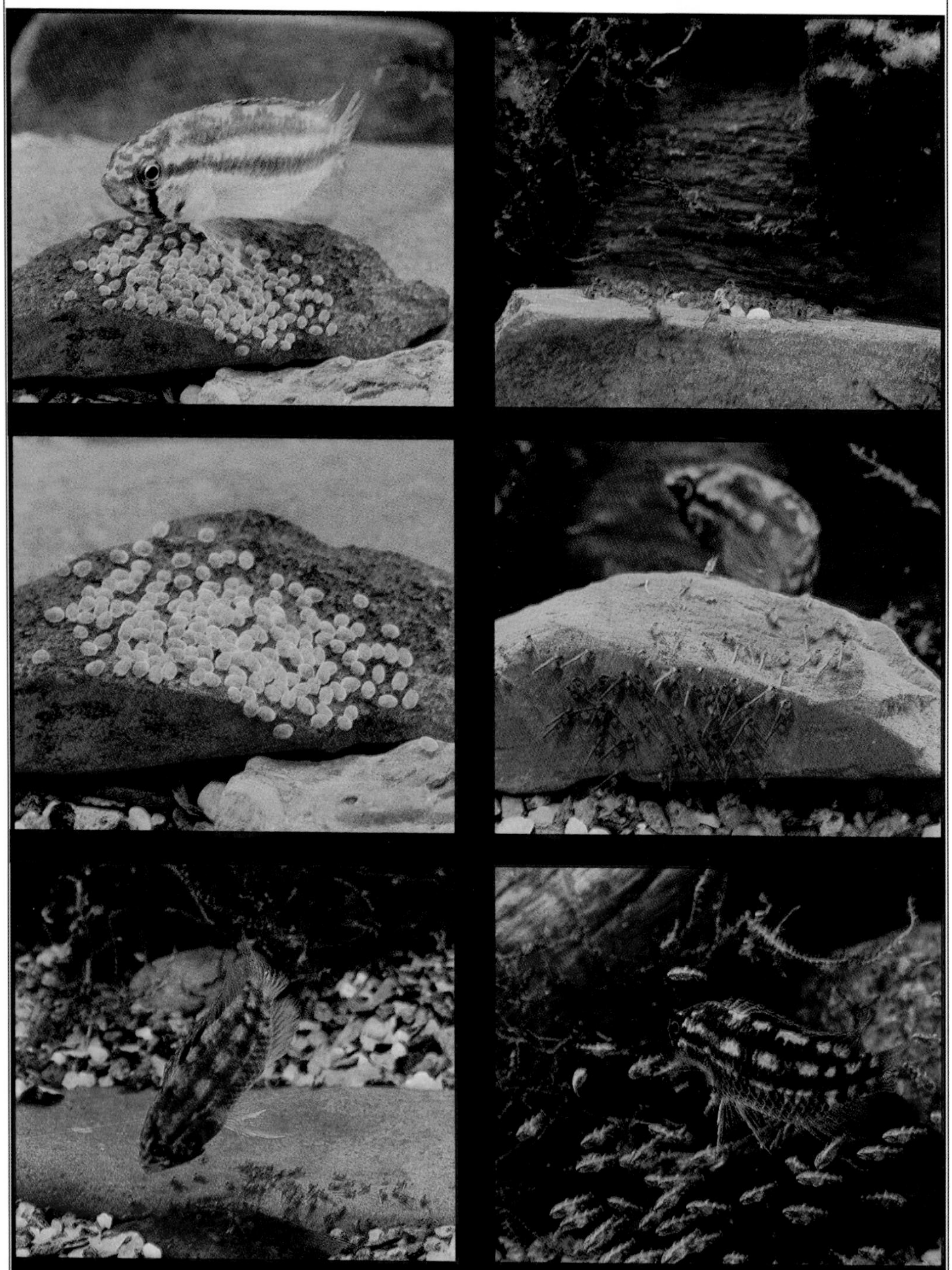

A spawning sequence showing the large amount of large eggs of *Nannacara anomala*, the newly hatched and free-swimming fry.

PHOTOS BY HANS JOACHIM RICHTER.

Scientific name: ***Pterophyllum scalare***
Popular name: **Angelfish**

This exotic fish is thought of as common now, but it certainly created a sensation when it was first imported early in the century. And you can bet that they were expensive then, as they had to be shipped in large containers by freighter all the way up from the Amazon. They were not easy to induce to spawn either, but their descendants, which have been captive-bred for many generations, are not so difficult. In contradistinction to most other cichlids, angelfish like to stay up in the water column, although they will pick up food from the bottom, looking unbelievably stately as they do so.

The angelfish species *Pterophyllum altum*.

PHOTO OF WILD FISH JUST COLLECTED BY DR. HERBERT R. AXELROD.

Angelfish of the normal wild-type color pattern, usually referred to as "regular" or "silver" angels.

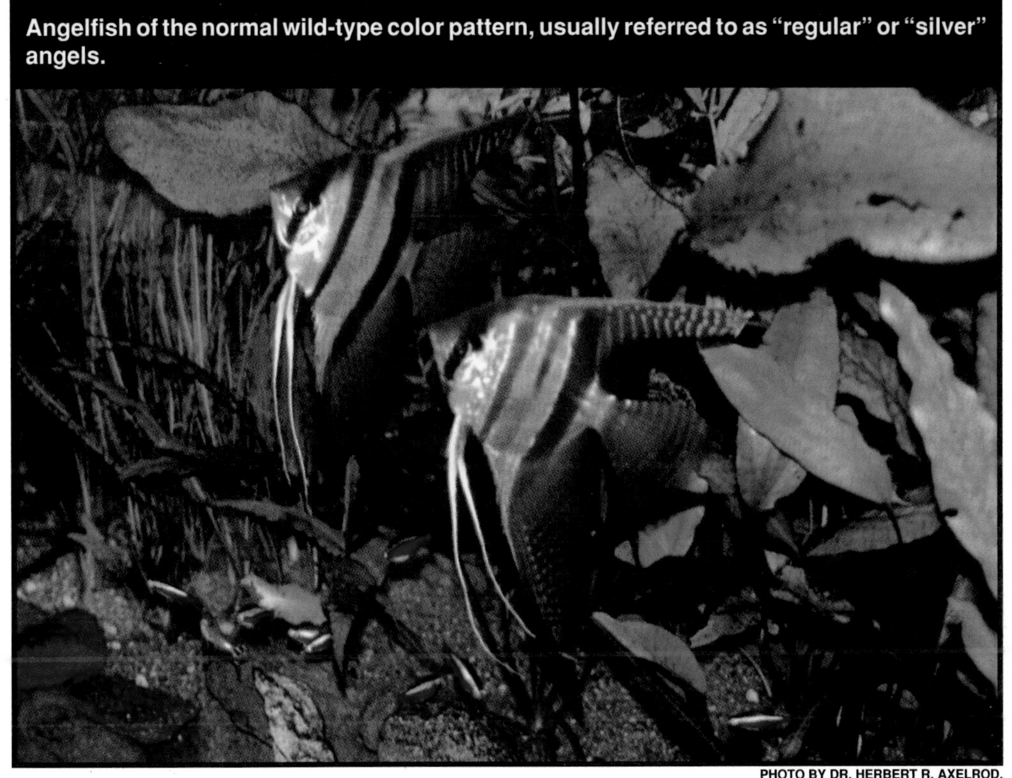

PHOTO BY DR. HERBERT R. AXELROD.

Angelfish spawn on plants or tree limbs in the wild. When the young hatch, they move them to other plants (instead of putting them in pits, as is the case with many other cichlids), and they transfer them from plant to plant. When the young are free swimming, they will take newly-hatched brine shrimp, and they are cared for by both parents. Unfortunately, angelfish are raised commercially by removing the eggs from the parents, so many parental angels may not be effective parents, since the bad ones have not been selected out in a Darwinian manner, as they would have in nature.

Although there are many fancy varieties which have been bred in the aquarium, including gold varieties, the natural form still looks the best to those of us who want our fish as they are found in nature. There are two other species in the genus, *P. altum* and *P. leopoldi*, but they are difficult to tell apart unless you have a practiced eye. The males and females in all three species are also quite similar in appearance, requiring an expert to tell them, and even the expert may be wrong half the time!

Pterophyllum leopoldi.

PHOTO BY A. MCFARLANE.

Three of the many kinds of discus hybrids.

PHOTO BY MP&C PIEDNOIR.

Scientific name: ***Symphysodon discus***
Popular name: **Discus**

Along with the angelfish, this species is generally considered the most exotic of tropical fish species, but many cichlidophiles (cichlid lovers) would disagree. There are believed to be at least two species of discus, with several subspecies. The other species is *Symphysodon aequifasciata*, but there are ichthyologists who will argue that there is only one species. In that case, it would be the above, as it was the first one described.

There are two types of discus hobbyist. The most common are the ones who breed fancy varieties. I am not in that camp myself, as I find most of the fancy varieties inane. For example, one fancy variety is an elongated type. Isn't that absurd? The charm of the fish was always its disk-like shape and majestic manner, and some crazy discus hobbyists decide the shape should be different. Oh well, if you like that sort of thing, I won't complain, but the other camp of discus hobbyists is the one I like the most. They want their discus as close to the wild types as possible, and they even make expeditions down to the Amazon to capture wild specimens for diversity in the captive genetic pool.

Of course, some cichlids are not to be kept in the typical community tank, as they would decimate their tankmates—especially when they spawned. But many of them are peaceful by cichlid standards, and they are covered in the next chapter.

Common discus spawning.

PHOTO BY C. SANDERS.

Symphysodon discus discus from the Rio Negro of Brazil.

PHOTOGRAPHED AND COLLECTED BY DR. HERBERT R. AXELROD.

CICHLIDS FOR THE SPECIAL TANK

In this case, "special" means a tank that has fish which are of a relatively large size and can take care of themselves. It doesn't mean that they have to be tough; they just have to be able to get out of the way. Tinfoil barbs and silver dollars are excellent examples of this category, although the South American purist would only keep silver dollars, since tinfoil barbs are not from the Amazon, or from South America, for that matter. If you are not that finicky, you can even keep smaller fishes, such as tiger barbs and zebra danios. These fish are all fast enough to swim out of trouble's way.

The other option, of course, is simply to keep a cichlid tank of cichlids that are of comparable aggression levels or that have a little extra size to help compensate for a lack of scrappiness. In any case, the following cichlids are not quite mild, but they aren't typically cichlid-aggressive either. While a lot of people bemoan the aggression of cichlids, I should point out that it has evolved as a component of cichlid behavior that helps them protect their young. In other words, what frustrates us about cichlids is the very thing that also endears them to us.

***Mylossoma duriventre*, a silver dollar, is a fast swimmer and successfully lives with cichlids.**

PHOTO BY HANS JOACHIM RICHTER.

***Brachydanio frankei*, the leopard danio, can live with cichlids because they are fast enough to escape them.**

PHOTO BY EDWARD TAYLOR.

***Capoeta tetrazona*, the tiger barb, can be kept with cichlids.**

PHOTO BY MARK SMITH.

Scientific name: *Acarichthys heckelii*
Popular name: Threadfinned Acara

This is a relatively hardy South American cichlid that can tolerate a wide variety of water conditions and feeds well on a variety of foods. However, spawning is not simple with this species in the home aquarium. For one thing, in the wild the females dig various chambers in the clay of the bottom or in the river banks. This creates a maze that predators must enter to reach the fry. The females actively solicit a mate once the chambers are ready, but she only wants him for fertilizing the eggs, then she drives him off. In the wild, the male presides over a harem and guards a large territory which includes all the females in his harem.

As can be imagined, it is difficult to reproduce such a setting in a tank. Some hobbyists have had success using lots of inverted clay pots of various sizes or using various sizes of PVC piping. For spawning, high temperatures are needed (85° to 90°), with lots of aeration and frequent partial water changes.

This species is closely allied to the eartheaters (*Geophagus*), which is a quite varied group and is in the process of revision by ichthyologists. The genus *Acarichthys* differs from the eartheater complex by the absence of a lobed gill arch.

Acarichthys heckeli.

PHOTO BY MP&C PIEDNOIR.

Scientific name: *"Aequidens" pulcher*
Popular name: Blue Acara

The genus *Aequidens* has been restricted recently to the larger members of the genus. It was long recognized that dissimilar fishes were included in the genus and that detailed study was needed to sort out the species. Unfortunately, this species is excluded from the genus, but no new genus has been erected for it (and the many species like it), so we are still sticking to the old generic name, but note that it is in quotes to make known the fact that the genus for this species will probably eventually change.

In any case, the blue acara has been a popular fish in the aquarium hobby for over sixty years. It has sometimes been referred to in the literature as *Aequidens latifrons*, which is a very similar species (and which also will need a new generic name). One of the reasons for the popularity of this fish is that it only attains a size of about five inches, and the fish are excellent parents, with both of them caring for the fry. They are ready spawners, tolerate a variety of water conditions, and they don't demand a huge territory, even when spawning, so they aren't overly tough on tankmates. Even so, they are not for the typical community tank, but they fit perfectly here.

Scientific name: *Biotodoma cupido*
Popular name: Cupid Cichlid

This species was described in 1840 as *Geophagus cupido*, but it has different technical structures

Aequidens pulcher.

PHOTO BY DR. HERBERT R. AXELROD

from that species. In any case, it is a cichlid that can reach about six inches in length, but it is quite peaceful. As is the case with most cichlids, the only time it causes problems is when spawning time arises. Of the species in this chapter, this is the one most demanding of good water quality and relatively soft water. I kept a group many years ago in my hard San Diego water, but I never got them to spawn. From what I know now, increased temperature and

Biotodoma cupido, the Cupid cichlid.

PHOTO BY AARON NORMAN.

soft water were what I needed. It is interesting to note that the small juvenile specimens were quite colorless, being basically a transparent white coloration with black markings. Upon reaching maturity, the fish developed iridescent colors that changed hues slightly as the fish turned in the light. A delicate and subtle beauty, this species needs a little extra care.

Cichlasoma bimaculatum.

PHOTO BY RAINER STAWIKOWSKI.

Scientific name: *Cichlasoma bimaculatum*
Popular name: Port Cichlid

The common name comes from the old name *Aequidens portalegrensis* by which the fish in the aquarium were known. (The true *portalegrensis* is now also known as a *Cichlasoma* species.) The species spawns very much like the blue acara, but it gets a little larger, with the males easily attaining six inches in length. The species was never striking or colorful, but they were "old reliables," in that they would spawn easily and would take excellent care of the young. So many of the American substrate spawning cichlid species have been reported to secrete a supplementary food for their young that the behavior can be assumed in most such species. Only moderately aggressive, this fish is a great first cichlid, along with the blue acara, for the budding cichlidophile to cut his teeth on.

It is interesting to note that this species and eleven other species very similar to it are what now are restricted to the genus *Cichlasoma* as revised by Sven Kullander in 1983.

Scientific name: *Crenicichla* species
Popular name: Pike Cichlid

Although the *Crenicichla* species are deadly ambush predators, many species make good aquarium residents for the special tank, the main requirement being that all members of the tank be too large too swallow. Although the fish are excellent parents, they aren't overly aggressive as most cichlids go. Once sexual maturity is reached, the males can be told from the females by their larger size (up to eight inches) and more

Crenicichla species, one of the pike cichlids.

PHOTO BY MARK SMITH.

spangles on the body. But the females have the best coloration, sporting a bright red in the belly region.

Nearly all of the *Crenicichla* species are cave spawners, and aquarists use flower pots and PVC piping to accommodate them. Although they are efficient fish predators, they will eat dry and frozen foods.

Scientific name: *Geophagus jurupari*
Popular name: Jurupari

The name jurupari is a native name, so it is not a patronym and is not pronounced with the long "i" at the end. This is one of those species that has undergone revision and has been placed in the genus *Satanoperca*. Because the species has been so well known by the old genus and that the name change may not be accepted by the ichthyological community in the long run, I have used the old name. It is only fair to say that the name change is accepted by many ichthyologists who know the species quite well. (It is my hope that those new to scientific names won't be put off by all of the name changes. The changes are a healthy sign in that they reflect that a lot of research and study is being done with these animals. Thus, the changes in names reflect a refinement of our scientific understanding of these fishes.)

Geophagus (Satanoperca) jurupari.

PHOTO BY MP&C PIEDNOIR.

These fish are amazingly adaptable to water quality and are found throughout the Amazon, but they have to deal with different water parameters in some coastal areas. This species can reach nearly a foot in length, but it takes it at least three years to do so. It is not aggressive with other cichlids, so its size helps protect it from some of the smaller more aggressive cichlids.

Scientific name: *Heros severus*
Popular name: Severum

The popular name comes from the days that this fish was called *Cichlasoma severum*. The species name was changed only to agree in gender with its new genus. The genus *Heros* is restricted to these types of cichlids. Utilization of the name for these cichlids really sabotaged those aquarists who used the next scientific name available in place of *Cichlasoma*,

Heros severus.

PHOTO BY MARK SMITH.

and it shows the pitfalls of using the next available name. (Some ichthyologists are using *Herichthys* for the cichlids that formerly were in the genus *Cichlasoma*, but *Herichthys* is quite likely to be restricted to the Texas cichlid. That is the reason that many ichthyologists and hobbyists still use *Cichlasoma* for species that are no longer included in that genus. However, quotation marks are often included around the generic name to indicate the problem of placement in a genus.)

Herichthys carpinte, the Texas cichlid.

PHOTO BY HANS JOACHIM RICHTER.

This species is relatively peaceful and a bi-parental substrate spawner. It has long been an aquarium favorite. The pink variety was in vogue for a while, but hobbyists soon learned that it was tough to improve on nature. The fish attains about eight inches in length. While this fish is not small by any means, it will seem quite small and mild when compared to the cichlids in the next chapter!

BIG OR BAD—OR BOTH!

It takes really dedicated aquarists to keep these fish, as they all get either very large or they are extremely aggressive. Some are both! Certain robust species are so aggressive that the hobbyist must put up a grid as a barrier to keep the cichlid from getting at the heater and smashing it to pieces. Cichlids with very aggressive behavior tend to "displace" some of the aggression by attacking objects in the tank. The grid used to protect the heater and other vulnerable equipment is usually the plastic grating used for diffusing big fluorescent lighting fixtures. Such material can also be used in attempting to breed some of these monsters. Believe it or not, the fish find a way to spawn with the grid between them.

Some people may wonder why anyone would want to keep such large and aggressive fish. The

Aequidens rivulatus.

PHOTO BY EDWARD TAYLOR.

answer is that it is these very fish that exhibit some of the most interesting behavior. Besides, their very aggression can be quite amusing. It is interesting that a behavior that has evolved for protecting a territory or the young of a fish can be so highly developed that the fish will actually show aggression toward large animals—such as its keeper!

Scientific name: *"Aequidens" rivulatus*
Popular name: Green Terror

Again, this is one of the species which was excluded from the new definition of *Aequidens*, so quotation marks are placed around the generic name. To add to the confusion, the true *"Aequidens" rivulatus* may not be the one that is extant in the tropical fish hobby. The other one is similar in appearance and disposition, but the other has more iridescent green scales and it hails from the Pacific slope, while the one in the hobby was collected in eastern Ecuador. The species reaches about ten inches in length, but it will spawn at a much smaller size, from five to six inches. The best way to spawn the fish is at that size, as you can obtain six individuals and let them pair up naturally. Otherwise, you will have to use a grid divider for a pair, as the large ones are hard to pair up.

Once the fish attain their ultimate size, you very likely may need the grating anyway to protect the heater and other important fixtures in the tank. A single member of the species may be kept as a pet all by itself in a tank, as these animals are quite intelligent and learn to recognize their owners and even perform tricks for food. You will need great patience for the latter activity, but I have seen it done. Large specimens are also at their best in appearance and coloration.

Interestingly, the original fish which were brought in and earned the name green terrors had vertical fins with ivory margins. If your fish have orange margins on the caudal, dorsal, and anal fins, they will be relatively peaceful as compared to the original green terrors—but they can still be a handful!

Obviously, these fish are extra trouble to keep, but the species is quite fascinating in behavior, and its beauty can be jaw dropping.

An albino *Astronotus ocellatus.*

PHOTO BY DR. HERBERT R. AXELROD.

Scientific name: *Astronotus ocellatus*
Popular name: Oscar

This species ranges widely across South America, and there may even be other species of the genus; in fact, there is one other nominal species, *Astronotus orbiculatus*, but it is difficult to tell from this species. This is one of the most popular of all cichlids in spite of its size. That is partly because the juveniles are so cute in appearance, and they beg for food and attention like puppies. But even the larger specimens are popular because they become quite pet-like. Also, a pair can live together peacefully in a hundred-gallon tank, and they are still quite pet-like with their owners, in contra-distinction to parrots which have a mate.

Oscars are popular because the babies are so cute. This species comes from the Rio Negro.

PHOTO BY MARK SMITH.

As a young hobbyist, I discovered that one could keep a juvenile oscar in the typical community tank, but this situation only lasts for a few weeks. Oscars grow quite rapidly. And while they are not aggressive, they are quite predatory on fishes that they can swallow. When I saw my cute little oscar baby carrying a neon tetra like a dog with a bone in his mouth, I knew that it was time to remove him to his own tank. Interestingly, these cichlids can be easily bullied by smaller cichlids, as they truly are not aggressive. One of the distinctions that cichlidophiles have to learn to make is the difference between predation and aggression. The fact is that many predatory fish are not aggressive.

Oscars have been popular for so long that many artificial color forms have been bred. There is a red form that is quite good looking and a "red tiger" coloration that isn't bad. But the natural colors are still the best to a true cichlidophile.

Although oscars are not nearly as aggressive as most other cichlids, a pair with young will attack a heater, so you will need some protection for it, such as the grating already discussed. Even an oscar by itself may knock out the heater from sheer size or in a sudden fit over perceived lack of attention from its owners. Some hobbyists provide a floating Ping Pong ball for them to play with. Just make sure that the fish hasn't become large enough to swallow it.

Even though oscars are specialized fish eaters, they learn to eat earthworms and dry food in captivity. They should have as much variety as possible. Clean water is important for these animals, so at least weekly 15% partial water changes should be made.

Scientific name: *Caquetaia spectabilis*

This fish, which reaches about 12 inches in length, is familiar to many hobbyists as "*spectabile.*" That is because the species was once known as *Cichlasoma*

Caquetaia spectabilis.

PHOTO BY ALF STAHLBURG.

spectabile, and the species name was changed to agree with the gender of the new generic name. At least, this species has its new genus. Although this species is not full of the personality that oscars are famous for, it is another large predator and may even be better looking once it gets its adult coloration. Like the oscar, the species is not aggressive, even though it is an ambush predator, much like the oscar. Like the oscar, it can't tolerate being in with the normal aggressive cichlids even though they may be smaller than it.

Scientific name: *Cichla ocellaris*
Popular name: Peacock Bass or Peacock Cichlid or Tucunare

Here is a fish whose popular name came from game fishermen. (Tucunare is the native name for the fish and is used by some hobbyists.) Apparently, fishing interests arranged for the species to be transplanted to Florida. This was a mistake, as it so often is when an exotic is transferred to another locale, as the peacock prospered at the expense of native fish species. Even though this cichlid is a candidate for the largest cichlid in the world (vying with the emperor cichlid, *Boulengerochromis microlepis*, of Lake Tanganyika), it is not an aggressive fish, and it should not be kept with aggressive cichlids that are anywhere near its size.

It is an ambush predator, and I have seen them in action enough to comment that it is quite impressive to see how fast these big fish can move once the prey gets within reach.

Obviously, this is only a fish for fanatics. Tanks are needed that are well over two hundred gallons of capacity. Further, the young are not easily trained to take anything other than live fish. Add to that the problem that the species is quite intolerant of less-than-perfect water and is more likely to come down with diseases than most other cichlids, and you get the idea that you really have to really like this type of cichlid to properly keep them.

Cichla ocellaris, the tucunaré.

PHOTO BY DR. HERBERT R. AXELROD.

Scientific name: *"Cichlasoma" festae*
Popular name: Red Terror

Here is another fish that takes a fanatic to keep it, but it brings enough attractive qualities to inspire such fanaticism. For one thing, a specimen in good condition can rival nearly any fish in majestic appearance and spectacular coloration. Second, the species has behavior that is not only fascinating but is downright spectacular. This is the type of fish that when it is defending its young will leap out of the water at a hand that is placed over the surface of where the fry are located! Still, a single specimen can be kept in a community tank of large and rough cichlids, but the tank should be quite large, at least two hundred gallons capacity. That doesn't mean that the fish can't be spawned, but it is best done when they are relatively small. Pairing at full size is quite tricky, for the fish reach a considerable size, easily ten inches in length, and they are quite formidable. I once placed an adult male and several females in a 250-gallon tank, thinking that a relatively safe situation. Since there were so many females for the male to choose from, I reasoned, he wouldn't single out one female for bullying. Well, I miscalculated that time. A pair formed almost immediately, and they turned their defenses on the other females, trying to drive them away. And they were dead on my return late that day.

A female red terror.
PHOTO BY MP&C PIEDNOIR.

As usual, the best way to get a pair for spawning is to invest in six young and let them grow up and pair up naturally. They will spawn at a size of less than six inches, but a full-grown compatible pair with young is quite a sight to behold. The huge, beautiful pair acts as though it will eat the dog if it comes close to the tank. And even the aquarist is tolerated within narrow parameters.

Although the fish is well worth keeping, it comes honestly by its name "red terror." That is, it truly is really red, nearly glowing with its own light when in full spawning color, and it is truly a terror, too, as a parental pair will countenance no fish in the same tank with them, regardless of the size of the tank. It and the green terror were first imported at about the same time from the same general locality, the eastern part of Ecuador.

CHOOSING SOUTH AMERICAN CICHLIDS

It has been frustrating to limit the enumeration of South American cichlid species for a book such as this, for there are so many of them. Further, there are a great many species that are excellent candidates for the home aquarium. On the other hand, I didn't want to leave out some of the big cichlids, for there is nothing quite like them for certain cichlid enthusiasts. And who is to deny them their "impractical animals" as long as they are willing to provide large enough quarters and are willing to go to the extra trouble to keep them?

But the frustration is leaving so many great species out. Just be aware that there are different species in nearly every genus I have mentioned. As just one example, I only mentioned one species of pike cichlid, but there are countless species, and they range from what could be called dwarf species to behemoths. I must confess that I was imprinted on the generalized cichlid, such as the green terror, red terror, or blue acara, and I tend to prefer those types of cichlids. Still, the specialized fish predator that the pike cichlids have become are quite fascinating. They are experiencing something of a boom in popularity among advanced cichlid hobbyists these days. Part of the reason for that is that there are so many species of them, and they vary so much in size and in color, not to mention in life habits. They epitomize how cichlids have been able to enter the realm of freshwater fishes and carve out special niches for themselves.

But the pike cichlids are only one example of specialization and cichlid success. The angels and discus are another, as is the quite similar *Uaru*, which I didn't even bother to mention. The point is that the pickings are extraordinary in the South American realm for the cichlid enthusiast. They are so good, in fact, that it is impossible to keep them all. So a decision must be made. What types to keep?

***Uaru amphiacanthoides*, an immature specimen.**

PHOTO BY MARK SMITH.

If you are a fish breeder with a cichlid hatchery, you might be tempted to keep the very same pike cichlids that I have discussed briefly here. And the market for

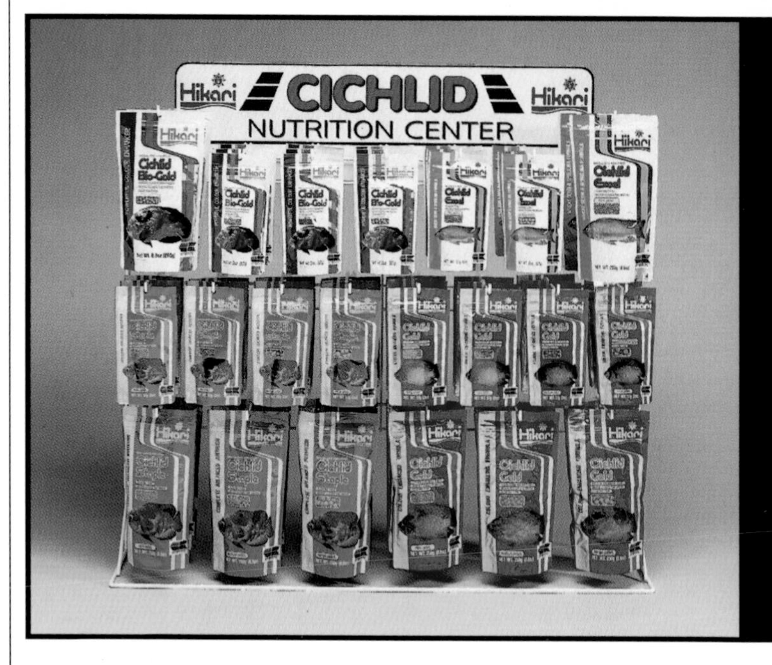

Cichlids have special nutritional requirements which may not be met by ordinary tropical fish diets. Special foods designed specifically for cichlids are available. Photo courtesy of Hikari Sales, USA

them would be pretty good right now, since they are so much in vogue. It should be mentioned, however, that these are a specialist's fish, so they wouldn't have the broad appeal of angels or rams. So economic demand is one criterion for deciding on what fish to keep, but that is relevant only if you have a hatchery (remembering that a cichlid hatchery can be as simple as a few tanks in the basement or as complicated as a separate building with an automatic water changing system for the tanks).

The best reason for choosing a variety of fishes is that you like them yourself. There are dedicated dwarf cichlid fans that wouldn't think of keeping some of their "ruffian" brethren. And there are those that keep some of the medium to large cichlids that hardly consider the idea of "practical" and "sensible" dwarf cichlids.

If you are a breeder of fishes and are thinking primarily in economic terms, angels, rams, oscars, and discus are always in demand. Even if you spawn fishes primarily for profit, you are undoubtedly inclined, to some extent at least, to pick species that appeal to you, too. So it will take some experience on your part at keeping all the different animals to decide on just what your type of cichlid is.

An important point worth noting is that somehow the cichlid hobbyists seem to have the most fun. That is not just my opinion, for it is not original with me. It was voiced once by the late great William T. Innes, and it has been expressed by numerous authorities since then. So pick your species and let them lead you where they will. The chances are that you will enjoy the ride and learn a little biology along the way!

INDEX

Page numbers in **boldface** refer to illustrations.